Cardiff

Travel Guide

Quick Trips Series

Table of Contents

Cardiff

Cardiff is the capital of Wales and is a vibrant, attractive

city of interest to tourists who are interested in Welsh

culture and history. During the summertime the city hosts

some fun outdoor festivals and makes the most of the

better weather with a fun al-fresco dining and bar scene.

CARDIFF TRAVEL GUIDE

Cardiff has an impressive history and has existed since Roman times. The Romans built the city and were followed by the Normans who built over it. The Vikings developed the city more given its strategic three rivers location. This ultimately brought much prosperity to Cardiff through maritime activities.

In the early 1800's the discovery of coal followed by the industrial revolution transformed the lives of the inhabitants again. At one point Cardiff was the biggest exporter of coal in the world and it was for this reason that Edward VII awarded it city status in 1905. In the year of 1913 more than 10 million tons of coal passed through the port.

As a city Cardiff is proud of its history, language and culture and the changes that been made over the past

2000 years. The Cardiff Story is a free museum that tells about this thriving and international city through the eyes of the local people. In 2004 Cardiff was named as the world's first Fair Trade capital city and in 2005 the centenary celebrations marked the start of a 12 month programme of event and festivities.

Many famous names have associations with Cardiff and it was from here that Captain Robert Scott set sail for the South Pole in 1910 in his ship Terra Nova. Children's author Roald Dahl was born in Cardiff and christened in the Norwegian Church that is now a café and arts centre. In the world of music Charlotte Church and Shirley Bassey are homegrown superstars.

By the 1970's and 1980's Cardiff was a city in decline and massive amounts of money were poured in to bring life back to this failing and unloved part of Wales. The plan

was to make it a place where people wanted to live and

businesses wanted to invest and the success of the city

shows the investments were justified. The dock area has

been regenerated and Cardiff Bay is now a bustling port

with a leisure development on the waterside.

The building of the multi-purpose Millennium Stadium was

an important part of helping with the transformation of

Cardiff into a true European capital. The Rugby World

Cup final was hosted at the Millennium Stadium in 1999

and Wales won the Six Nations Grand Slam

Championship in 2005, 2008 and 2012. In 2009 Cardiff

hosted the first test for the Ashes cricket as well as

various football matches during the London 2012

Olympics

CARDIFF TRAVEL GUIDE

The social scene of Cardiff includes traditional pubs, cosy bars, and funky nightclubs and a myriad of restaurants. Visitors can choose from eating out in establishments that have been awarded 2 AA rosettes and serve the finest produce, to every kind of fast food imaginable or cosy pubs serving traditional Welsh food.

In the city centre head for Mill Lane and sip a cocktail or two and people-watch or go to Cardiff Bay and hang out on the waterfront. Eastside in St David's is known as the dedicated restaurant quarter where there are cuisines and prices to suit all tastes and pockets spread over two floors.

Welsh lamb, Welsh Black Beef, Camarthen ham abound and to wash it all down there is Welsh wine and whisky as well as beautiful spring water fresh from the mountains.

Bara Brith, Welsh cakes and cawl are very popular and a popular breakfast item is Laver bread made from boiled seaweed.

Shopaholics will be pleased to know that Cardiff has been named as the 6th best destination in the UK for shopping. There are all kinds of shopping opportunities; ultra-modern shopping centres offer everything under one roof while the pretty Victorian and Edwardian arcades have a bit more character and more individual shops, not chain stores.

Customs & Culture

The entertainment and culture in Cardiff is varied and diverse. There is a range of ballet, operas, musicals and live music from local and international acts. There are

CARDIFF TRAVEL GUIDE

galleries, art museums, theatres and many venues, some small and intimate, others that can seat many thousands.

Cardiff is a Centre of Culture and this is reflected by the striking Wales Millennium Centre. The city's art and culture economy is showcased every year by Creative Cardiff who promote many events and festivals that take place every year.

One of the major art events in the city is the biennial Artes Mundi Exhibiton Prize where national and international artists compete over a 12 week period for a prize worth £40,000

Every July the International Food and Drink Festival takes over the Cardiff Bay area. This is heaven for food lovers as over one hundred stalls offering wines, cheeses, liqueurs, seafood and fish from all over the world come together in this delightful waterfront setting. There is free entertainment with a programme that includes soul, jazz, country and western, folk and skiffle so just relax and enjoy the good times.

As July rolls into August Cardiff Bay becomes alive with the Cardiff Festival. All things nautical plus watersports and tall ships bring colour and vibrancy to the city and the waterfront area. There are also many fishy events like the Fish Craft Championships. The Continental market has a range of alternative foods for anyone not that keen on food from the oceans and rivers.

The Cardiff Festival is the largest free outdoor festival in the UK and everywhere events take place. There is street theatre, live music, funfairs, children's entertainment and of course lots of places to eat and drink.

🌍 Geography

Cardiff is the youngest capital city in Europe and situated in South Wales and occupies a relatively flat area mainly on reclaimed marshland. To the west, east and north the city is surrounded by hills rising to just over 1,000 feet above sea-level. It is these geographic features that earned Cardiff its position as the world's largest coal port, due to ease of access to the south Wales coalfields and proximity to the seas.

As well as being the Welsh capital Cardiff is the county town of Glamorgan and the ninth largest city in the UK. The urban population is estimated to be around 350,000. As an alternative destination for tourists Cardiff ranks as number six in the world according to National Geographic magazine and welcomes 18 million visitors annually.

The University of Cardiff attracts students not just from Wales and the UK but from all over the world and many foreign languages can be heard in the city centre. The city has grown economically with great success over the past 10 years and has reached a level of competitiveness above the UK average.

There are still some parts of Cardiff that haven't yet benefitted from the success of the city. To the west of the city are some of the largest housing estates in the UK. The Ely housing estate in particular is an economically disadvantaged area but the people have a tight knit community and are working hard to improve their lives and surroundings.

CARDIFF TRAVEL GUIDE

The Welsh people are keen to keep their native language alive and learning Welsh is compulsory at school until the age of 16. Only 11% of Cardiffians speak Welsh compared to the 19% national average.

Transport links are excellent with international flights from Cardiff Airport going to 30 European destinations and long haul flights departing from Heathrow some 90 minutes away. Cardiff Airport is 10 miles from the city centre in the village of Rhoose and regular bus and rail services connect the airport to their respective stations in the city centre.

Road links are great and Cardiff is a couple hours from London on the M4. Many drivers use the M48 Severn

CARDIFF TRAVEL GUIDE

Bridge crossing to enter Wales or the M4 Second Severn

Crossing both of which have a toll fee payable.

Cardiff Central railway station is the largest in Wales and

10 million passengers a year pass through its seven

platforms. Trains from here leave for long distance

services to Holyhead and Wrexham as well as London,

Manchester, Edinburgh and Glasgow. Cardiff Queen

Street station is the hub for the Valley Lines that connect

the suburbs and further out into the South Wales valleys.

The trains for Cardiff Bay leave from Queen Street

station.

For cyclists and walkers the 55 miles of the Taff Trail runs

from Cardiff Bay to the Brecon Beacons National Park.

Nearly the entire path is off-road, following disused

railways lines and paths alongside the River Taff. The

Brecons Bike Bus on Sundays takes cyclists out to Brecon so they can ride back to Cardiff.

🌍 Weather & Best Time to Visit

Cardiff is within the northern temperate zone and has a maritime climate with mild weather that is often wet and windy with many clouds.

In the winter it rains quite a lot with December being the wettest month. The daytime temperature hovers around 8°C falling to 2°C at night.

The seasons of spring and autumn are fairly similar with rain showers likely at any time. The daytime highs can reach 18°C and drop quite sharply to a chilly 4°C through the night.

CARDIFF TRAVEL GUIDE

Summer in Cardiff is sunniest in July with many hours of sunshine. The driest months are April to July but it will still rain at some point. When it rains it might only be a short shower rather than the downpours that are typical the rest of the year. The mercury can reach 21°C if the sun comes out and drop back down to 11°C in the evenings.

A holiday in Wales any time of year means packing for all kinds of weather. It is more than likely to rain so a decent jacket and umbrella are handy to have. Even in summer a cardigan or jumper for the evenings is worth taking along as there is nothing worse than enjoying a meal out and being cold. For hiking or trekking in the Welsh Mountains a sturdy pair of boots and thick socks can prevent blisters.

Sights & Activities: What to See & Do

🌐 Cardiff Castle

Castle St, Cardiff, CF10 1BT

Tel: +44 29 2087 8100

www.cardiffcastle.com/

Cardiff Castle is right in the heart of the city centre and

was built in the 11th century by the Normans on top of a 3rd century Roman fort.

There is a lot to see at the castle including the lavishly decorated Castle Apartments. The ceilings in the apartments are quite spectacular as is the library with its floor to ceiling bookshelves. There are Wartime Shelters, The Norman Keep and the Battlement Walk to go round and absorb over 2000 years of history.

The grounds are immaculate and ideal for taking a stroll through. There is a café for light refreshments with panoramic views of the city and surrounding countryside. All through the year events take place at the castle such as jousting, open air theatre and medieval parties.

The castle is open from 9am to 5pm daily and an adult ticket costs £11 with slight discounts for children and concessions.

Techniquest Science Museum

Stuart St

Cardiff

CF10 5BW

Tel: +44 29 2047 5475

www.techniquest.org/

Techniquest is in the heart of Cardiff Bay and is an interactive science and discovery centre. A giant red Welsh dragon welcomes visitors to the 120 hands-on exhibits.

There are huge chunky puzzles, a science theatre, a discovery room with fossils and forensics and the amazing digital Planetarium. Where else is it possible to fire a giant pop gun, launch a rocket and study ant colonies?

There are programmes of event and workshops for families at weekends and during school holidays. Local school groups benefit by all these exciting exhibits with term-time visits.

In Café Quest lunches and light snacks are available and the Techniquest shop has gifts and souvenirs. The centre is disabled friendly to all parts of the building and there are hearing loops in the Planetarium and in the Science Theatre.

Techniquest is open 10am to 5pm at weekends, bank holidays and seven days a week through school holidays. During term-time the opening hours are Tuesday to Friday 9.30am to 4.30pm. An adult ticket costs £7 and children pay £5.

Doctor Who Experience

Discovery Quay, Porth Teigr, Butetown, Cardiff

CF10 4GA

Tel: +44 844 801 3664

www.doctorwhoexperience.com/

The creator of the infamous "dalek" was born in Cardiff so where better to have an exhibition dedicated to the famous Doctor.

CARDIFF TRAVEL GUIDE

The BBC Studios at Cardiff Bay is where much of the series is filmed as well as on location in the city.

Next door to the TV studios the Doctor Who Experience takes visitors on a spectacular journey through time and space, able assisted by a Sonic Screwdriver of course. Squeeze through a crack in time and help the Doctor face his enemies, fly the TARDIS and meet some of the scariest monsters ever. The special effects in the exclusive action-packed sequences will amaze fans and families alike.

There is a collection of Doctor Who costumes from 1963 to the present day as well as many original artefacts and props. Interactive experiences allow visitors to discover how the special effects are created and how the shows are filmed.

CARDIFF TRAVEL GUIDE

There is plenty to see and do plus a huge range of Doctor Who goodies to buy in the gift shop. The Experience is open 9.30 to 5pm daily in the school holidays and every day except Tuesdays in term-time.

An adult ticket costs £15 and children pay £11. There are special merchandise packs available for adults and children at the cost of £36.50 and £32.50 respectively including T-shirt, postcards and other exciting Doctor Who goodies. Family tickets are available and buying tickets online does make a small saving.

For fans who want to see where the shows are filmed the Doctor Who Tour of Cardiff Locations is a three hour bus tour in and around the city. There is more information on www.britmovietours.com/

🌏 Red Castle

Castell Coch

Tongwynlais

Cardiff

CF15 7JS

Tel: +44 29 2081 0101

Lots of us would love to own a castle but not many of us have the money or determination to follow that dream. One lucky individual who did just that was the third Marquis of Bute. On a steep hillside high above the village of Tongwynlais to the north of Cardiff is Castell Coch or Red Castle.

This fairy tale castle with its three towers was rebuilt by Bute in the 19th century on the ruins of the original Red Castle which had been constructed six centuries earlier.

The newer castle is brightly lit and the wooden trimmings and moveable drawbridge are painted a reddish-orange colour in keeping with the name. The original castle was built of red sandstone with red roof tiles but the tiles that protect the castle now from the elements are green, but infinitely more durable.

The Keep Tower is the most spectacular part of the castle and on the lower level is the Drawing Room. The octagonal ceiling is stunning with vaulting and bright colours. Floral patterns and birds as well as many small animals decorate the walls and ceilings mixed in with starry skies.

The castle is cared for by Cadw, the Welsh Government's historic service and is open to the public Monday to Saturday 10am to 4pm and from 11am on Sunday. Adults pay £4.50 with slight reductions for children and concessions. There is a small café serving light refreshments as well as a gift shop.

Millennium Stadium

Westgate St

Cardiff

CF10 1NS

Tel: +44 870 013 8600

www.millenniumstadium.com/

The Millennium Stadium is one of the most well-known icons of modern Wales and a tour of this sports venue is an exciting part of a visit to Cardiff. The Millennium Stadium has a fully retractable roof in case the sun shines and the only pitch system where the turf can be removed so other events can take place without causing any damage to the grass.

Visitors can see where all the action takes place on match days and get behind the scenes. The experienced tour guides will take you round the stadium where you can visit the Press Conference Suite and the dressing room of the Welsh team; the Dragon's Lair.

As you walk down the player's tunnel towards the pitch the roar of the 74,500 fans is deafening and there is a certain thrill in stepping out onto the immaculately kept turf. The tour ends with a view of the pitch from a VIP hospitality suite and then onto the President's Box. This is the box normally reserved for royalty but just for a few brief seconds visitors can lift the trophy and be a sporting superstar.

Tours can be booked online and take place Monday to Saturday from 10am to 5pm and on Sunday from 10am to 4pm. £9.50 and children pay £6.00.

🌐 Cardiff International White Water Centre

Watkiss Way

Cardiff

CF11 0SY

Tel: +44 29 2082 9970

www.ciww.com/

Cardiff International White Water, CIWW, is full of action packed activities for all the family to enjoy, and get wet of course. White water rafting on a variable flow river, kayaking, hot dogging, river boarding and hydro-speeding are some of the exciting sports to try. Whether you are an expert or a beginner there is something for everyone to have a go at.

For the less adventurous there is a flat water area where gentle kayaking can be enjoyed or just sit back and relax on the café balcony. The balcony overlooks the river so spectators can watch the watery fun and games going on below them.

All the necessary equipment is provided to take part in any activity and there is a Canoe and Kayak Store selling specialised equipment. Session times and prices vary according to age and activity; there is comprehensive information on the CIWW website or give the centre a call.

CIWW is closed on Monday but open from 9am the rest of the week. Closing times are Tuesday, Thursday and Saturday 5pm, Wednesday and Friday 8pm and Sunday 4pm.

🌐 Norwegian Church

Harbour Drive, Cardiff Bay, Cardiff, CF10 4PA

Tel: +44 29 2087 7959

www.norwegianchurchcardiff.co.uk/

When Cardiff was one of the world's great exporters of coal the town was desperately in need of timber. The Norwegian ships brought strong Scandinavian timber to be used as pit props in the mines and in return took coal back to Norway. The Norwegian Church is now an Arts Centre but it was originally a church for Norwegian sailors.

The church was consecrated in 1868 and became known as a welcome point for Norwegian sailors, offering food and friendship in a strange country. The hospitality quickly extended to all sailors and between 1867 and 1915 the number of visiting seaman rose from 7,572 to 73,580 per annum.

Roald Dahl was baptized in the church and the first floor art gallery bears his name. On the ground floor the Grieg Room is the main hall where various events take place. The Norsk Café is open daily and there are delicious cakes and treats to try, many of them with a Norwegian flavour.

The Norwegian Church is open seven days a week from 9.30am to 5pm and admission is free.

🌐 Cardiff Metropolitan Cathedral

38 Charles St

Cardiff

CF10 2SF

Tel: +44 29 2023 1407

www.cardiffmetropolitancathedral.org.uk/

The Metropolitan Cathedral of Cardiff is also known as St David's Cathedral and is a Roman Catholic cathedral in the heart of Cardiff. It is the focal point of Catholic life in Cardiff and is only one of three Roman Catholic Cathedrals in the UK associated with a choir school.

There are three choirs; Boys, Junior Girls and Senior Girls. The choirs have performed in Paris, Bruges,

Denmark and Amiens as well as in episodes of Doctor Who and for BBC Radio Wales

The cost of building the cathedral in 1842 was the princely sum of £2,124, most of which was donated by benefactors or raised by well-wishers.

The cathedral is open daily from 8am to 6pm with slightly later closing on Saturday and Sunday of 7pm. Admission is free.

National Museum & Art Gallery

Cathays Park

Cardiff

CF10 3NP

Tel: +44 29 2057 3000

CARDIFF TRAVEL GUIDE

www.museumwales.ac.uk/

The National Museum of Wales was established in 1907 but the collections in the 15 galleries tell the story of art in Wales and Europe from the last 500 years. The beautiful scenery of Wales has inspired artists of many types and there are not only paintings in the museum but collections of furniture and silver as well.

Two sisters Gwendoline and Margaret Davies generously gave their magnificent personal collections to the museum. These collections were exceptional and contained sculptures and paintings by Cézanne, Monet, Rodin and Millet. There is also a stunning collection of porcelain donated by Wilfred Seymour De Winton and some unrivalled local ceramics gifted to the museum by Ernest Morton Nance.

In the Prints and Drawing Room there are 28,000 works and a selection of these can be viewed by arrangement. There are three studios for art conservation and a workshop to take care of the framing of pictures and care and maintenance of the collections.

For a welcome sit down and some refreshments there is the Oriel Restaurant where hot and cold lunches and snacks can be purchased. The restaurant is family friendly and serves children's portions and has high chairs available. The Coffee Shop in the Main Hall has a good selection of sandwiches and homemade cake and hot and cold drinks. The shop has gifts to suit all tastes; from pocket money souvenirs to beautiful pieces of art.

The National Museum and Art Gallery is open Tuesday to Sunday from 10am to 5pm and admission is free.

St Fagan's Natural History Museum

Cardiff, CF5 6XB

Tel: +44 29 2057 3500

www.museumwales.ac.uk/

The Natural History Museum is situated in the grounds of the beautiful and historic St Fagan's castle. It is the most popular heritage site in Wales and one of Europe's leading outdoor museums. The 100 acre site was donated to the people of Wales by the Earl of Plymouth and opened to the public in 1948.

More than 40 of the original buildings have been restored and among them are a Workmen's Institute, a farm, a chapel and a school. Workshops and demonstrations by local craftspeople bring the site to life and quite often the results of their endeavours are on sale. Farming demonstrations are given and in the verdant pasture land native breeds graze happily.

There several choices of places to eat at St Fagan's or you can bring a picnic and take advantage of the beautiful grounds. Café Bardi serves sandwiches, soups, salads and cakes. The Gwali Tea Rooms is decorated in traditional 1930's style and serves delicious light lunches and afternoon teas. A recently opened food outlet is Yr Odyn serving hot and cold food and this is on the site of the old pottery.

Locally made ice-cream is available in all the food outlets and at various locations throughout the park. The Museum bakery sells bread and cakes to take away.

St Fagan's is open daily from 10am to 5pm and admission is free. Car parking costs £3.50 per day.

🌐 Rhondda Heritage Park

Trehafod

Rhondda

South Wales

Tel: +44 1443 682 036

www.rhonddaheritagepark.com/

Rhonda Heritage Park is 20 miles or so from Cardiff city centre and can easily be reached by car, bus or train. There is a railway station at Trehafod and the trains leave

CARDIFF TRAVEL GUIDE

from Cardiff Central Station. A one way journey costs

about £5.

This famous tourist attraction gives an insight into life as

part of a coal mining community which still existed well

into the 1980's. This was one of the world's most

important mining areas for coal and at one time there

were 53 working collieries in an area only 16 miles long.

The Underground Experience Tour takes about 40

minutes and once you have put your safety helmet on one

of the guides will take you down in the lift cage to the

bottom of the pit. For a short time visitors can begin to

imagine what life must have been like underground. The

life was very hard, with the men hardly ever seeing

daylight, especially in the winter months. Facing hazards

and doing strenuous tasks hundreds of feet below the surface were part of a normal day for a miner.

On the ground floor of the visitor centre there is a reconstruction of a village street from days gone by showing commercial and domestic life in the Valleys. On the first floor the Art Gallery and Café offer the opportunity to have a bite to eat overlooking the Rhondda Valleys spread out below. The exhibitions in the gallery are always changing and displays of jewellery, ceramics and artworks can be viewed.

Children visiting the mine today are much luckier than they would have been when the mine was in operation. Today youngsters can enjoy playing in the Energy Zone and not have to worry about being sent to work down the pit from the age of eight years old. Some would have started even younger as trappers at the tender age of just five. This was a vitally important job and the children were responsible for opening and closing the trap doors to allow the fresh air to flow through.

The admission price for adults is £3.50 and just £2.50 for children. This is for entrance to the Underground Experience Tour and the Energy Zone. Entry to the visitor centre, café and Art Gallery is free. In the gift shop there is an affordable range of souvenirs relating to the mine and Rhondda Valleys as well as Welsh costumes for children and rugby shirts and scarves.

In September each year the Giant Veg Show comes to the Rhondda Heritage Park. For two days local growers strive to win prizes with their enormous vegetables. Not just the biggest, but the heaviest and ugliest vegetables are all welcome in this free event. There are also cooking

demonstrations and gardening tips.

Open daily 9am to 4.30pm with free admission.

Wales Millennium Centre & Welsh National Opera

Bute Place

Cardiff

CF10 5AL

Tel: +44 29 2063 5000

www.wmc.org.uk/

www.wno.org.uk/

Millennium Centre

The Millennium Centre was opened in 2004 by Her

Majesty the Queen and is one of the liveliest and unique

centres for performing arts in Europe. The exterior as visitors approach is striking and has been featured in the Doctor Who and Torchwood series.

There are events for all the family including West End Musicals, hip hop and ballet, contemporary dance and stand-up comedy. The website has excellent information regarding all the shows and many of them are free, just turn up on the day and watch.

There are bars and restaurants ranging from Foyer Bars for those pre-performance and interval drinks to the Hufen ice cream parlour. The Crema coffee shop has to be the place to relax in for anyone that likes coffee culture. For bistro food and fine drinks in a contemporary setting Bar One is open to for casual visitors and theatre goers

CARDIFF TRAVEL GUIDE

For a full meal or a snack ffresh Bar and Restaurant is committed to using the freshest of local produce prepared and cooked by highly qualified chefs. The restaurant has been featured in the Michelin Guide and The Good Food Guide.

The gift shop in the Millennium Centre has some traditional souvenirs of Wales and also some more unusual ones. Gift certificates and gift memberships are an ideal way to introduce friends or family to the magic of the centre.

Adopt A Slate. The face of the centre is made up of Welsh slate hewn from Blaenau Ffestiniog and Machynlleth and in keeping with the industrial past of Wales. For £75 a slate can be adopted and every adopter receives a certificate and gets the chance to name their slate.

Take Your Seat. In the Donald Gordon Theatre this is a slightly more expensive but wonderful gift or can be purchased in memory of a loved one. For £500 a plaque will be engraved and put in situ on one of the seats in the theatre. Welsh celebrities such as Michael Ball and Max Boyce have already done this so you will be in good company.

Welsh National Opera

The Welsh National Opera is housed inside the Millennium Centre and is an ideal place to go and learn about this wonderful world of music and dance.

Many people see opera as boring, outdated and something that you have to wear long dresses and posh suits for. At the Welsh National Opera there isn't a dress code so jeans and trainers are fine but if you want to

dress up to the nines that is ok as well.

The word opera is the Italian word for work and an opera

is simply a story told through words and music. An opera

differs from a musical in that normally microphones are

not used and the orchestra is much bigger and always

plays live.

For opera beginners some of the most popular are

Madam Butterfly and Tosca, both by Puccini, La Traviata

by Verdi and The Magic Flute by Mozart.

To get the most out of an opera especially for the first visit

it is sometimes good to do a little research beforehand on

the story.

Budget Tips

🌐 Accommodation

The River House

59 Fitzhamon Embankment, Cardiff, CF11 6AN

Tel: +44 29 2039 9810

www.riverhousebackpackers.com/

River House is a small family run hostel on the banks of

the River Taff.

CARDIFF TRAVEL GUIDE

This is an excellent location close to the central bus and train stations as well as many of Cardiff's attractions. The hostel has been featured in the New York Times as well as the top daily UK newspapers.

There are 12 bedrooms with a mix of twin beds, four or six beds and female only rooms. There are free lockers and the rooms are cleaned daily. Sheets and duvets are included but not towels. A buffet breakfast is included in the room price as well as free Wifi.

There is a guest lounge with comfy settees for chatting to fellow guests, DVD hire for when the weather is not so great and a fully equipped kitchen for making light meals.

There is a member of staff available 24 hours a day and a very friendly cat that does like sleeping on beds. The price per night per person including breakfast starts at £15 depending on the time of year.

Nomad Backpacker Hostel Cardiff

11-15 Howard Gardens

Cardiff

CF24 0EF

Tel: +44 29 2025 6826

www.nomadcardiff.co.uk/

The Nomad Hostel welcomes backpackers from all over the world who want to come and stay in the heart of Cardiff.

CARDIFF TRAVEL GUIDE

The hostel is 10 minutes from the Millennium Stadium and half that time to the lively city centre. For late night owls and party goers St Mary's Street is where the young and thirsty head for. After all that booze a takeaway is a must and Caroline Street is also called Chip Alley for reasons that will be obvious to anyone visiting.

There are no minimum two night stays or curfews at the Nomad so visitors can come and go as they please. Safety is important to us and there is 24 hour CCTV in the social areas and staff on duty 24 hours as well.

There is a whole range of facilities at the Nomad including a free breakfast to get the day off to a good start. The rooms are a mixture of dorms, including all female ones. There are free lockers, linen, hot showers and shower gels, Wifi access and in the TV room there is free movie access. There is a licensed bar to meet like-minded travellers, a games room, a kitchen for guests and a laundry room.

Prices start at £12 per person per night in a shared dorm.

Austins Guesthouse

11 Coldstream Terrace, Cardiff

Cf11 6LJ

Tel: +44 29 2037 7148

www.hotelcardiff.com/

The two large buildings at numbers 11 and 9 Coldstream Terrace are just 300 yards from Cardiff Castle and are home to Austins.

CARDIFF TRAVEL GUIDE

There are 11 rooms in total sleeping up to 20 guests. There are a variety of singles, twins and doubles, some with shared bathroom facilities and some ensuite. The superior rooms and apartment have a kitchenette with kettle, toaster and microwave. All the rooms are bright and linen and towels are provided as well as Freeview TV, free Wifi and a workstation area.

There is a light and bright lounge for guests to enjoy with SKY TV and games and books to borrow. A smart decked terrace is a lovely place to enjoy a pre-dinner drink or a nightcap.

For guests with cars parking is possible outside or there is a small car park at the rear of the property. Breakfast isn't included but can be purchased at the guesthouse with a choice of a full breakfast of a lighter option.

CARDIFF TRAVEL GUIDE

Prices start at £30 per room per night for a basic single room and £44 per room per night for a basic double room.

Hotel One Hundred

100 Newport Road

Cardiff

CF24 1DG

Tel: +44 7916 888 423

www.hotelonehundred.com/

More boutique hotel than B&B the Hotel One Hundred offers a place to stay in Cardiff city centre that is chic, stylish and affordable.

The seven elegant bedrooms are all furnished with comfortable beds, crisp linen and fluffy pillows for a good night's sleep. All the rooms have ensuite facilities with complimentary toiletries, flat screen TV, free Wifi, hospitality tray and access to a fridge and microwave.

For guests that would like to enjoy some super leisure time the hotel owners have organised an exclusive deal with a four star local hotel. Guests of the Hotel One Hundred can use the fitness and leisure club for just £8 per person.

A twin ensuite room for two guests including breakfast starts at £50 and a triple ensuite from £75. A substantial continental style buffet breakfast is included and for a small extra charge a full English breakfast can be ordered.

The Big Sleep Hotel

Bute Terrace

Cardiff

CF10 2FE

Tel: +44 29 20 636363

www.thebigsleephotel.com/

This hotel opened in 1999 in a blaze of publicity due to it being co-owned by actor John Malkovich. It is close to the Motorpoint Arena and the new St David's shopping centre and the bars and restaurants of the Café Quarter are a short distance away for sampling the best of Cardiff nightlife.

The hotel has 81 bedrooms all ensuite with free Wifi, hospitality tray, flat screen TV and ensuite bathrooms.

58

CARDIFF TRAVEL GUIDE

There are a variety of rooms to suit all needs from the Penthouse and Executive Suites with separate lounges to the smart and welcoming twin or double rooms. Prices start from £29 per room per night. There are several rooms available for disabled guests.

The idea of the hotel is simple; to deliver good value accommodation with a small price tag. The hotel appeals to not just leisure guests but business travellers and families as well. The hotel will also accept the family dog for a small charge.

A complimentary light breakfast is included which can be eaten at the hotel or is available as a takeaway for anyone in hurry There is a 24 hour reception and free parking on a first come, first served basis and the Lobby Bar has refreshments and light snacks.

🌐 Restaurants, Cafés & Bars

Katiwok

53 Crwys Road, Cathays, Cardiff, CF24 4ND

Tel: +44 29 2037 6222

www.katiwok.co.uk/

The first thing you will notice when you visit Katiwok is the unusual décor. It is decorated with lime green chairs screaming for attention over the shocking pink ones!

The food is cheap and good and the restaurant has won awards from the Observer and the Guardian newspapers. The walls are covered in photos and the brightly coloured menus offer a selection of Pan Asian street food.

There are deliciously spicy noodles and fried rice, as well as Afghan chicken, Filipino seafood, Asian beef and a whole lot more to choose from. There are drinks and desserts and some great meal deals and Katiwok is licensed so beer and wine is available.

Katiwok is open Tuesday to Thursday noon until 2.30pm and 5pm to 10.30pm, Friday noon until 2.30pm and 5pm to 11.30pm, Saturday noon until 11.30pm and Sunday noon until 10.30pm.

Old Cottage Lisvane

Cherry Orchard Road

Lisvane

Cardiff

CF14 0UE

Tel: +44 29 2076 5961

CARDIFF TRAVEL GUIDE

www.oldcottagecardiff.co.uk/

The Old Cottage in Lisvane is the quintessential country pub. The character of the pub is everywhere, in the cosy corners to the roaring fires and the unique dining room. In the summer months the garden is a delight with scattered seating areas for guests to enjoy.

The menu ranges from traditional dishes such as fish and chips, to delicious steaks with prime Welsh beef and fresh pasta and pizza.

The produce used in the kitchen is locally sourced and the chef's take great care when preparing the menus. The menus are seasonal and Mediterranean flavours are interwoven with British influences. Fixed price menus from

£11.50 tempt the taste buds and on Sunday the choice of roast is unbelievable.

The Potted Pig

27 High Street

Cardiff

CF10 1PU

Tel: +44 29 2022 4817

www.thepottedpig.com/

Just a stone's throw from the Millennium Stadium and Cardiff Castle and hidden away in a bank vault under the city of Cardiff is the Potted Pig. The curved ceiling and concealed lighting add a harmonious and romantic atmosphere to this unusual setting.

CARDIFF TRAVEL GUIDE

Modern British food is served but with a hint of French flavours and New York grill style cooking. The menus are seasonal and the food comes from local independent suppliers.

The signature dish of Potted Pig with toast and pickles for a starter is different, followed by one of the exciting and unusual main courses such as Whole roast Poussin with bread sauce, sprouts & bacon & truffle chips.

Fine wines and drinks match the menus and there is an unrivalled range of spirits particularly of bespoke gins.

The Potted Pig is open for lunch Tuesday to Sunday from noon to 2pm. Dinner is served Tuesday to Thursday between 7pm and 9pm and Friday and Saturday 6.30pm to 9.30pm. The restaurant is closed all day Monday and

Sunday evenings.

K2

23 High St

Cardiff

CF5 2DY

Tel: +44 29 2056 3637

This little café serves up decent sandwiches, jacket

potatoes and light lunches. It does get busy through the

week at lunchtimes as many local people pop in for

takeaways. The staff will make up any sandwich no

matter how bizarre the filling and the prices are

reasonable. K2 serves a decent breakfast and is open

from 8am to 5pm Monday to Saturday.

Trade Street Café

4 Trade Street

Cardiff

CF10 5DQ

Tel: +44 29 2022 8666

www.tradestreetcafe.com

The Trade Street café is hidden in a warren of offices and arty studios and has a regular clientele who crowd in to buy wraps, sandwiches, cakes and breakfasts. Daily specials are good old-fashioned food like beef and ale pie, chips and gravy for about £6.

The food is all cooked on the premises using locally sourced ingredients. The honey roasted ham is roasted in-house and thick pink slices of this delicious meat can be tried in the Croque Madame filled with creamy Welsh cheddar.

Simple but comforting desserts like sticky toffee pudding, scones with cream and jam and of course Welsh cakes are the ideal way to round off a meal. The café is open Monday to Friday from 7.30am to 3.30pm.

🌐 Shopping

Cardiff Market

St Mary Street

Cardiff

CF1 2AU

Tel: +44 29 2087 1214

www.cardiff-market.co.uk/

This impressive Victorian structure with a massive glass

roof is home to Cardiff Market. The market has been trading since the 1700's and although the farmers no longer tie their sheep, cows and goats outside some of the features from times gone by still exist. Originally the site of Cardiff's gaol the gallows were situated where the St Mary's Street entrance is today.

The market sells just about everything, from nuts and bolts to jams and jewellery, fruit and vegetables, fresh meat, fish and clothes. There are haberdashery stalls where ribbons, buttons and bows of every shape and colour can be purchased, stalls with walking sticks and records old and new.

The market is loud, colourful and bustling but that is what markets are all about. The market is open Monday to Saturday from 8am to 5.30pm.

St David's Shopping Centre

Mary Ann Street

Cardiff

CF10 2EQ

Tel: +44 29 2036 7600

www.stdavidscardiff.com/

The shopping centre of St David's in Cardiff has enough shops to satisfy even the fussiest shopper. There are top name stores selling outfits for all occasions as well as home ware and electronics. The Apple store has all the latest gadgetry while the John Lewis store is the largest store in the chain outside of London.

The double level Grand Arcade is nearly 800 feet in length which is long enough to fit in 24 double decker buses. The restaurant quarter known as Eastside also covers two floors and offers a wide choice of bars, restaurants, cafés and fast food outlets inside the centre. For more alfresco dining Hayes Boulevard has a super selection of eateries.

Opening hours are Monday to Friday 9.30 to 8pm, Friday 9.30 to 7pm and Sunday 11am to 5pm.

Castle Welsh Crafts

1-3 Castle St

Cardiff CF10 1BS

Tel: +44 29 2034 3038

www.castlewelshcrafts.co.uk/

A visit to Cardiff would not be complete without taking home some reminders of time spent in Wales.

CARDIFF TRAVEL GUIDE

The Castle Welsh Crafts shop has a vast range of gifts and mementos of Wales.

The business was started by the Rice family over 35 years ago and is still owned and run by the family. The founder's daughter is director and keeps a strict eye on the business and the customer service and goods offered.

Whether you want a cuddly red Welsh dragon or a lovespoon to give to someone special there is a super choice of items in the shop. Miners lamps, gifts made from slate and Welsh jewellery are some of the beautiful items available. For sporty fans rugby shirts in all sizes can be bought as well as T-shirts with witty Welsh slogans, braces, ties and aprons.

Madam Fromage

21-25 Castle Arcade

Cardiff CF10 1BU

Tel: +44 29 2064 4888

www.madamefromage.co.uk/

Madam Fromage is an amazing cheese shop and deli in the heart of Cardiff. A daily selection of over 150 cheeses from high quality specialist suppliers will tantalise the taste buds as soon as you enter the shop. Daily deliveries from Rungis in France and regular trips to cheese producers in Brittany and France means the shop has cheeses that are not normally available in the UK.

A good way to try some of the delicious cheeses is to join in one of the regular Cheese and Wine Events. The history of cheese, talks on cheese and cheesy jokes are the order of the day followed by a small buffet with drinks and music. It is a great way to make some like-minded friends and get to know some new cheeses.

The opening hours are Monday to Friday 10am to 5.30pm, Saturday 9.30am to 5.30pm and Sunday noon to 5pm.

Mermaid Quay

Cardiff Bay

Tel: +44 29 2048 0077

www.mermaidquay.co.uk/

Mermaid Quay is a shopping and leisure overlooking Cardiff Bay.

The waterfront setting is home not just to places to eat, drink and watch live entertainment but also to shops for clothes, fabulous furnishings, delicious foods and great gifts. There is the also an award winning hair-dressing salon and spa.

Bute Street stretches back towards the city centre from Mermaid Quay and along here are exciting little boutiques selling everything from Welsh cakes and typical Welsh souvenirs to modern art galleries, a bank, estate agent and betting shop.

An exciting way to travel to Mermaid Quay from the city centre is by Aquabus. The Hydro craft is a quick and fun way to make the journey. The Aquabus has level access and is suitable for disabled or elderly passengers as well as families with children. www.aquabus.co.uk

CARDIFF TRAVEL GUIDE

🌍 Entry Requirements

Citizens of the European Union do not need a visa when visiting the UK. Non-EU members from European countries within the European Economic Area (EEA) are also exempt. This includes countries like Iceland, Norway, Liechtenstein and Switzerland. Visitors from Canada, Australia, Japan, Malaysia, Hong Kong SAR, New Zealand, Singapore, South Korea and the USA do not need a visa to visit the UK, provided that their stay does not exceed 6 months. Visitors from Oman, Qatar and the United Arab Emirates may apply for an Electronic Visa Waiver (EVW) via the internet, if their stay in the UK is less than 6 months. You will need a visa to visit the UK, if travelling from India, Jamaica, Cuba, South Africa, Thailand, the People's Republic of China, Saudi Arabia, Zimbabwe, Indonesia, Cambodia, Nigeria, Ghana, Kenya, Egypt, Ethiopia, Vietnam, Turkey, Taiwan, Pakistan, Russia, the Philippines, Iran, Afghanistan and more. If you are in doubt about the status of your country, do inquire with officials of the relevant UK Embassy, who should be able to advise you. Visitors from the EU (European Union) or EEA (European Economic Area) will not require immigration clearance when staying in the Isle of Man, but may require a work permit if they wish to take employment there. If needed, a visa for the Isle of Man may be obtained from the British Embassy or High Commission in your country. Applications can be made via the Internet.

CARDIFF TRAVEL GUIDE

If you wish to study in the UK, you will need to qualify for a student visa. There are a number of requirements. First, you have to provide proof of acceptance into an academic institution and available funding for tuition, as well as monthly living costs. A health surcharge of £150 will be levied for access to the National Health Service. Applications can be made online and will be subject to a points based evaluation system.

If you need to visit the UK for professional reasons, there are several different classes of temporary work visas. Charity volunteers, sports professionals and creative individuals can qualify for a stay of up to 12 months, on submission of a certificate of sponsorship. Nationals from Canada, Australia, Japan, Monaco, New Zealand, Hong Kong, Taiwan and the Republic of Korea can also apply for the Youth Mobility Scheme that will allow them to work in the UK for up to two years, if they are between the ages of 18 and 30. Citizens of Commonwealth member countries may qualify for an ancestral visa that will enable them to stay for up to 5 years and apply for an extension.

CARDIFF TRAVEL GUIDE

Health Insurance

Visitors from the European Union or EEA (European Economic Area) countries are covered for using the UK's National Health Service, by virtue of a European Health Insurance Card (EHIC). This includes visitors from Switzerland, Liechtenstein, the Canary Islands and Iceland. The card can be applied for free of charge. If you are in doubt about the process, the European Commission has created phone apps for Android, IPhone and Windows to inform European travellers about health matters in various different countries.

Bear in mind that a slightly different agreement is in place for Crown Dependencies, such as the Isle of Man and the Channel Islands. There is a reciprocal agreement between the UK and the Isle of Man with regards to basic healthcare, but this does not include the option of repatriation, which could involve a considerable expense, should facilities such as an Air Ambulance be required. If visiting the UK from the Isle of Man, do check the extent of your health insurance before your departure. A similar reciprocal agreement exists between the UK and the Channel Islands. This covers basic emergency healthcare, but it is recommended that you inquire about travel health insurance if visiting the UK from the Channel Islands.

CARDIFF TRAVEL GUIDE

The UK has a reciprocal healthcare agreement with several countries including Australia, New Zealand, Barbados, Gibraltar, the Channel Islands, Montserrat, Romania, Turkey, Switzerland, the British Virgin Islands, the Caicos Islands, Bulgaria, the Falkland Islands and Anguilla, which means that nationals of these countries are covered when visiting the UK. In some cases, only emergency care is exempted from charges. Reciprocal agreements with Armenia, Azerbaijan, Belarus, Georgia, Kazakhstan, Kyrgyzstan, Moldova, Russia, Tajikistan, Turkmenistan, Ukraine and Uzbekistan were terminated at the beginning of 2016 and no longer apply.

Visitors from non European countries without medical insurance will be charged 150 percent of the usual rate, should they need to make use of the National Health Service (NHS). Exemptions exist for a number of categories, including refugees, asylum seekers. Anyone with a British work permit is also covered for health care. Find out the extent of your health cover before leaving home and make arrangements for adequate travel insurance, if you need additional cover.

Travelling with pets

If travelling from another country within the EU, your pet will be able to enter the UK without quarantine, provided that certain entry requirements are met. The animal will need to be microchipped and up to date on rabies vaccinations. This means that the vaccinations should have occurred no later than 21 days before your date of departure. In the case of dogs, treatment against tapeworm must also be undertaken before your departure. You will need to carry an EU pet passport. If travelling from outside the EU, a third-country official veterinary certificate will need to be issued within 10 days of your planned departure. Check with your vet or the UK embassy in your country about specific restrictions or requirements for travel with pets.

In the case of cats travelling from Australia, a statement will need to be issued by the Australian Department of Agriculture to confirm that your pet has not been in contact with carriers of the Hendra virus. If travelling from Malaysia, you will need to carry documentation from a vet that your pet has tested negative for the Nipah virus within 10 days before your departure. There are no restrictions on pet rodents, rabbits, birds, reptilians, fish, amphibians or reptiles, provided that they are brought from another EU country. For pet rabbits and rodents from countries outside the European Union, a four month quarantine period will be required, as well as a rabies import licence. Entry is prohibited for prairie dogs from the USA and squirrels and rodents from sub-Saharan Africa.

🌐 Airports, Airlines & Hubs

Airports

London, the capital of England and the UK's most popular tourist destination is served by no less than 6 different airports. Of these, the best known is **Heathrow International Airport (LHR)**, which ranks as the busiest airport in the UK and Europe and sixth busiest in the world. Heathrow is located about 23km to the west of the central part of London. It is utilized by more than 90 airlines and connects to 170 destinations around the world. The second busiest is **Gatwick Airport (LGW)**, which lies 5km north of Crawley and about 47km south of the central part of London. Its single runway is the world's busiest and in particular, it offers connections to the most popular European destinations. From 2013, it offered travellers a free flight connection service, called Gatwick Connect if the service is not available through their individual airlines. **London Luton Airport (LTN)** is located less than 3km from Luton and about 56km north of London's city center. It is the home of EasyJet, the UK's largest airline, but also serves as a base for Monarch, Thomson Airlines and Ryanair. **London Stansted Airport (STN)** is the fourth busiest airport in the UK. Located about 48km northeast of London, it is an important base for Ryanair and also utilized by EasyJet, Thomas Cook Airline and Thomson Airways. **London Southend Airport (SEN)** is located in Essex, about 68km from London's central business area. Once the third busiest airport in London, it still handles air traffic for EasyJet and Flybe. Although **City Airport (LCY)** is the nearest to the city center of London, its facilities are compact and limiting. The short runway means that it is not really equipped to handle large aircraft and the airport is not operational at night either. It is located in the Docklands area, about 6.4km from Canary Wharf and mainly serves business travellers. Despite these restrictions, it is still the 5th busiest airport in London and 13th busiest in Europe.

The UK's third busiest airport is **Manchester International Airport (MAN)**, which is located about 13.9km southwest of Manchester's CBD. **Birmingham Airport (BHX)** is located 10km from Birmingham's CBD and offers connections to domestic as well as international destinations. **Newcastle International Airport (NCL)** is located about 9.3km from Newcastle's city center and offers connections to Tyne and Wear, Northumberland, Cumbria, North Yorkshire and even Scotland. **Leeds/Bradford Airport (LBA)** provides connections to various cities in the Yorkshire area, including Leeds, Bradford, York and Wakefield. **Liverpool International Airport (LPL)**, also known as Liverpool John Lennon Airport, serves the north-western part of England and provides connections to destinations in Germany, France, Poland, the Netherlands, Spain, Greece, Cyprus, the USA, the Canary

Islands, Malta, Jersey and the Isle of Man. **Bristol Airport (BRS)** provides international access to the city of Bristol, as well as the counties of Somerset and Gloucestershire. As the 9th busiest airport in the UK, it also serves as a base for budget airlines such as EasyJet and Ryanair. **East Midlands Airport (EMA)** connects travellers to Nottingham.

Edinburgh Airport (EDI) is the busiest in Scotland and one of the busier airports in the UK. Its primary connections are to London, Bristol, Birmingham, Belfast, Amsterdam, Paris, Frankfurt, Dublin and Geneva. Facilities include currency exchange, a pet reception center and tourist information desk. **Glasgow International Airport (GLA)** is the second busiest airport in Scotland and one of the 10 busiest airports of the UK. As a gateway to the western part of Scotland, it also serves as a primary airport for trans-Atlantic connections to Scotland and as a base for budget airlines such as Ryanair, Flybe, EasyJet and Thomas Cook. **Cardiff Airport (CWL)** lies about 19km west of the city center of Cardiff and provides access to Cardiff, as well as the south, mid and western parts of Wales. In particular, it offers domestic connections to Glasgow, Edinburgh, Belfast, Aberdeen and Newcastle. **Belfast International Airport (BFS)** is the gateway to Northern Ireland and welcomes approximately 4 million passengers per year. **Kirkwall Airport (KOI)** was originally built for use by the RAF in 1940, but reverted to civilian aviation from 1948. It is located near the town of

Kirkwall and serves as gateway to the Orkney Islands. It is mainly utilized by the regional Flybe service and the Scottish airline, Loganair. The airports at **Guernsey (GCI)** and **Jersey (JER)** offer access to the Channel Islands.

Airlines

British Airways (BA) is the UK's flag carrier airline and was formed around 1972 from the merger of British Overseas Airways Corporation (BOAC) and British European Airways (BEA). It has the largest fleet in the UK and flies to over 160 destinations on 6 different continents. A subsidiary, BA CityFlyer, manages domestic and European connections. British Airways Limited maintains an executive service linking London to New York. The budget airline EasyJet is based at London Luton Airport. In terms of annual passenger statistics, it is Britain's largest airline and Europe's second largest airline after Ryanair. With 19 bases around Europe, it fosters strong connections with Italy, France, Germany and Spain. Thomas Cook Airlines operates as the air travel division of the Thomas Cook group, Britain and the world's oldest travel agent. Thomson Airways is the world's largest charter airline, resulting from a merger between TUI AG and First Choice Holidays. The brand operates scheduled and chartered flights connecting Ireland and the UK with Europe, Africa, Asia and North

America. Founded in the 1960s, Monarch Airlines still operates under the original brand identity and maintains bases at Leeds, Birmingham, Gatwick and Manchester. Its primary base is at London Luton Airport. Jet2.com is a budget airline based at Leeds/Bradford, which offers connections to 57 destinations. Virgin Atlantic, the 7th largest airline in the UK, operates mainly from its bases at Heathrow, Gatwick and Manchester Airport.

Flybe is a regional, domestic service which provides connections to UK destinations. Covering the Channel Islands, Flybe is in partnership with Blue Islands, an airline based on the island of Guernsey. Blue Islands offers connections from Guernsey to Jersey, London, Southampton, Bristol, Dundee, Zurich and Geneva. Loganair is a regional Scottish airline which is headquartered at Glasgow International Airport. It provides connections to various destinations in Scotland, including Aberdeen, Edinburgh, Inverness, Norwich and Dundee. Additionally it operates a service to the Shetland Islands, the Orkney Islands and the Western Islands in partnership with Flybe. BMI Regional, also known as British Midland Regional Limited, is based at East Midlands Airport and offers connections to other British destinations such as Aberdeen, Bristol and Newcastle, as well as several cities in Europe.

CARDIFF TRAVEL GUIDE

Hubs

Heathrow Airport serves as a primary hub for British Airways. Gatwick Airport serves as a hub for British Airways and EasyJet. EasyJet is based at London Luton Airport, but also maintains a strong presence at London's Stansted Airport and Bristol Airport. Manchester Airport serves as a hub for the regional budget airline Flybe, as does Birmingham Airport. Thompson Airways maintain bases at three of London's airports, namely Gatwick, London Luton and Stansted, as well as Belfast, Birmingham, Bournemouth, Bristol, Cardiff, Doncaster/Sheffield, East Midlands, Edinburgh, Exeter, Glasgow, Leeds/Bradford, Manchester and Newcastle. Jet2.com has bases at Leeds/Bradford, Belfast, East Midlands, Edinburgh, Glasgow, Manchester and Newcastle. Glasgow International Airport serves as the primary hub for the Scottish airline, Loganair, which also has hubs at Edinburgh, Dundee, Aberdeen and Inverness.

Sea Ports

As the nearest English port to the French coast, Dover in Kent has been used to facilitate Channel crossings to the European mainland for centuries. This makes it one of the busiest passenger ports in the world. Annually, 16 million passengers,

2.8 million private vehicles and 2.1 million trucks pass through its terminals. Three ferry services to France are based on the Eastern dock, connecting passengers to ports in Calais and Dunkirk. Additionally, the Port of Dover also has a cruise terminal, as well as a marina.

The Port of Southampton is a famous port on the central part of the south coast of the UK. It enjoys a sheltered location thanks to the proximity of the Isle of Wight and a tidal quirk that favours its facilities for bulky freighters as well as large cruise liners. The port serves as a base for several UK cruise operators including Cunard, Celebrity Cruises, P&O Cruises, Princess Cruises and Royal Caribbean. Other tour operators using its terminals include MSC Cruises, Costa Cruises, Crystal Cruises and Fred. Olsen Cruise Lines. Southampton is a popular departure point for various cruises to European cities such as Hamburg, Rotterdam, Amsterdam, Le Havre, Bruges, Barcelona, Lisbon, Genoa and Scandinavia, as well as trans-Atlantic destinations such as Boston, New York and Miami. A short but popular excursion is the two day cruise to Guernsey. Southampton also offers ferry connections to the Isle of Wight and the village of Hythe. The port has four cruise terminals and is well-connected by rail to London and other locations in the UK.

Eurochannel

The Eurotunnel (or the Channel Tunnel) was completed in 1994 and connects Folkestone in Kent with Coquelles near Calais. This offers travellers a new option for entering the UK from the European continent. Via the Eurostar rail network, passengers travelling to or from the UK are connected with destinations across Europe, including Paris, Brussels, Frankfurt, Amsterdam and Geneva. On the UK side, it connects to the London St Pancras station. Also known as St Pancras International, this station is one of the UK's primary terminals for the Eurostar service. The Eurotunnel Shuttle conveys private and commercial vehicles through the tunnel and provides easy motorway access on either side.

🌏 Money Matters

Currency

The currency of the UK is the Pound Sterling. Notes are issued in denominations of £5, £10, £20 and £50. Coins are issued in denominations of £2, £1, 50p, 20p, 10p, 5p, 2p and 1p. Regional variants of the pound are issued in Scotland and Northern Ireland, but these are acceptable as legal tender in other parts of the UK as well. The Isles of Jersey, Guernsey and

Man issue their own currency, known respectively as the Jersey Pound, the Guernsey Pound and the Manx Pound. However, the Pound Sterling (and its Scottish and Northern Irish variants) can also be used for payment on the Isle of Man, Jersey and Guernsey.

Banking/ATMs

ATM machines, also known locally as cashpoints or a hole in the wall, are well distributed in cities and larger towns across the UK. Most of these should be compatible with your own banking network, and may even be enabled to give instructions in multiple languages. A small fee is charged per transaction. Beware of helpful strangers, tampering and other scams at ATM machines. Banking hours vary according to bank group and location, but you can generally expect trading hours between 9.30am and 4.30pm.

Credit Cards

Credit cards are widely accepted at many businesses in the UK, but you may run into smaller shops, restaurants and pubs that do not offer credit card facilities. Cash is still king in the British pub, although most have adapted to credit card use. For hotel bookings or car rentals, credit cards are essential. Visa and MasterCard are most commonly used. Acceptance of American Express and Diners Club is less widespread. Chip and PIN cards are the norm in the UK. While shops will generally have card facilities that can still accept older magnetic strip or US chip-and-signature cards, you will find that ticket machines and self service vendors are not configured for those types of credit cards.

Tourist Tax

A tourist tax of £1 for London has been under discussion, but to date nothing has been implemented. The areas of Cornwall, Brighton, Edinburgh, Westminster and Birmingham also considered implementing a tourist tax, but eventually rejected the idea.

Claiming back VAT

If you are not from the European Union, you can claim back VAT (or Value Added Tax) paid on your purchases in the UK. The VAT rate in the UK is 20 percent, but to qualify for a refund, certain conditions will have to be met. Firstly, VAT can only be claimed merchants participating in a VAT refund program scheme. If this is indicated, you can ask the retailer for a VAT 407 form. You may need to provide proof of eligibility by producing your passport. Customs authorities at your point of departure from the European Union (this could be the UK or another country) will inspect the completed form as well as your purchased goods. You should receive your refund from a refund booth at the airport or from the refund department of the retailer where you bought the goods.

Tipping Policy

It is customary to tip for taxis, restaurants and in bars where you are served by waiting staff, rather than bartenders. The usual rate is between 10 and 15 percent. Some restaurants will add this automatically to your bill as a service charge, usually at a rate of 12.5 percent. Tipping is not expected in most pubs, although you may offer a small sum (traditionally the price of a half pint), with the words "and have one yourself". Some hotels will also add a service charge of between 10 and 15 percent to your bill. You may leave a tip for room-cleaning staff upon departure. Tip bellboys and porters to express your gratitude for a particular service, such as helping with your luggage or organizing a taxi or booking a tour. Tipping is not expected at fast food, self service or takeaway outlets, but if the food is delivered, do tip the delivery person. You may also tip a tour guide between £2 and £5 per person, or £1 to £2 if part of a family group, especially if the person was attentive, engaging and knowledgeable. In Scotland, most restaurants do not levy a service charge and it is customary to tip between 10 and 15 percent. Tipping in Scottish pubs is not necessary, unless you were served a meal.

Connectivity

Mobile Phones

Like most EU countries, the UK uses the GSM mobile service. This means that visitors from the EU should have no problem using their mobile phones, when visiting the UK. If visiting from the USA, Canada, Japan, India, Brazil or South Korea, you should check with your service provider about compatibility and roaming fees. The US service providers Sprint, Verizon and U.S. Cellular employ the CDMA network, which is not compatible with the UK's phone networks. Even if your phone does use the GSM service, you will still incur extra costs, if using your phone in the UK. For European visitors the rates will vary from 28p per minute for voice calls and 58p per megabyte for data. The alternative option would be to purchase a UK sim card to use during your stay in the UK. It is relatively easy to get a SIM card, though. No proof of identification or address details will be required and the SIM card itself is often free, when combined with a top-up package.

The UK has four mobile networks. They are Vodafone, O2, Three (3) and EE (Everything Everywhere), the latter of which grew from a merger between Orange and T-Mobile. All of these do offer pay-as-you-go packages that are tailor made for visitors. Through EE, you will enjoy access to a fast and efficient 4G network, as well as 3G and 2G coverage. There is a whole range of pay as you go products, which are still part of the Orange brand. These have been named after different animals, each with a different set of rewards. The dolphin package, which includes free internet and free texts will seem ideal to most tech savvy travellers. The canary plan offers free calls, texts and photo messages, while the raccoon offers the lowest call rate. Also through EE, you can choose from three different package deals, starting from as little as £1 and choose whether to favour data or call time.

With the Three packages, you will get a free SIM with the All-in-One package of £10. Your rewards will include a mix of 500Mb data, 3000 texts and 100 minutes calltime. It is valid for 30 days. Through the O2 network, you can get a free SIM card, when you choose from a selection of different top-up packages, priced from £10. As a service provider, O2 also offers users an international SIM card, which will enable you to call and text landline as well as mobile numbers in over 200 countries. With Vodafone, you can choose between a mixed top-up package that adds the reward of data to the benefit of voice calls and data only SIM card offer. The packages start at £10.

Alternately, you could also explore the various offers from a range of virtual suppliers, which include Virgin Mobile, Lebara Mobile, Lycamobile, Post Office Mobile and Vectone Mobile. Virtual Packages are also available through the retailers Tesco and ASDA.

Dialling Code

The international dialling code for the UK is +44.

Emergency Numbers

General Emergency: 999
(The European Union General emergency number of 112 can also be accessed in the UK. Calls will be answered by 999 operators)
National Health Service (NHS): 111
Police (non-emergency): 101

CARDIFF TRAVEL GUIDE

MasterCard: 0800 056 0572

Visa: 0800 015 0401

🌐 General Information

Public Holidays

1 January: New Year's Day (if New Year's Day falls on a Saturday or Sunday, the 2nd or 3rd of January may also be declared a public holiday).

17 March: St Patrick's Day (Northern Ireland only)

March/April: Good Friday

March/April: Easter Monday

First Monday in May: May Day Bank Holiday

Last Monday in May: Spring Bank Holiday

12 July: Battle of the Boyne/Orangemen's Day (North Ireland only)

First Monday of August: Summer Bank Holiday (Scotland only)

Last Monday of August: Summer Bank Holiday (everywhere in the UK, except Scotland)

30 November: St Andrew's Day (Scotland only)

25 December: Christmas Day

26 December: Boxing Day

(if Christmas Day or Boxing Day falls on a Saturday or Sunday, 27 and/or 28 December may also be declared a public holiday)

Time Zone

The UK falls in the Western European Time Zone. This can be calculated as Greenwich Mean Time/Co-ordinated Universal Time (GMT/UTC) 0 in winter and +1 in summer for British Summer Time.

Daylight Savings Time

Clocks are set forward one hour at 01.00am on the last Sunday of March and set back one hour at 02.00am on the last Sunday of October for Daylight Savings Time.

School Holidays

In the UK, school holidays are determined by city or regional authorities. This means that it could vary from town to town, but general guidelines are followed. There are short breaks to coincide with Christmas and Easter, as well as short mid terms for winter (in February), summer (around June) and autumn (in

October). A longer summer holiday at the end of the academic year lasts from mid July to the end of August.

Trading Hours

For large shops, trading hours will depend on location. There are outlets for large supermarket chains such as Asda and Tesco that are open round the clock on weekdays or may trade from 6am to 11pm. In England and Wales, the regulations on Sunday trading are set according the size of the shop. While there are no restrictions on shops less than 280 square meters, shops above that size are restricted to 6 hours trading on Sundays and no trading on Christmas or Easter Sunday. Post office trading hours vary according to region and branch. Most post offices are open 7 days a week, but hours may differ according to location.

In Scotland, the trading hours for most shops are from 9am to 5pm, Monday to Saturdays. In larger towns, urban city areas and villages frequented by tourists, many shops will elect to trade on Sundays as well. Some rural shops will however close at 1am on a weekday, which would usually be Wednesday or Thursday. Some shops have introduced late trading hours on Thursdays and longer trading hours may also apply in the summer months and in the run-up to Christmas. On the Scottish islands of Lewis, Harris and North Uist, all shops will be closed on a Sunday.

Driving Policy

In the UK, driving is on the left side of the road. Both front and rear passengers must wear seat belts. If travelling with children, they must be accommodated with an age-appropriate child seat. With rental cars, it is advisable to make prior arrangements for this when you arrange your booking. If stopped by the police, you may be asked for your driver's licence, insurance certificate and MOT certificate, which must be rendered within 7 days. Driving without insurance could result in the confiscation of your vehicle.

In urban and residential areas, the speed limit for all types of vehicles is 48km per hour. On motorways and dual carriageways, cars, motorcycles and motor homes less than 3.05 tonnes are allowed to drive up to 112km per hour. On a single carriageway, this drops to 96km per hour. For motorhomes above 3.05 tonnes and vehicles towing caravans or trailers, the speed limit is 80km for single carriageways and 96km for dual carriageways and motorways. Local speed limits may vary. The alcohol limit for drivers is 35mg per 100ml of breath in England

and Wales and 22mg per 100ml of breath in Scotland (or 80mg and 50mg respectively per 100ml of blood).

Drinking Policy

The legal age for buying alcohol in the UK is 18. Young persons of 16 to 17 may drink a single beer, cider or glass of wine in a pub, provided they are in the company of an adult. From the age of 14, persons can enter a pub unaccompanied to enjoy a meal and children are allowed in pubs with their parents until 9pm. For buying alcohol at an off-license, you will need to be over 21 and may be asked to provide identification.

Smoking Policy

In the UK, smoking is prohibited in public buildings, all enclosed spaces and on public transport. Smoking is also prohibited at bus shelters. The law also states that 'no smoking' signage must be displayed clearly within all premises covered by the legislation. The only exceptions are rooms specifically designated as smoking rooms.

CARDIFF TRAVEL GUIDE

Electricity

Electricity: 230 volts

Frequency: 50 Hz

The UK's electricity sockets are compatible with the Type G plugs, a plug that features three rectangular pins or prongs, arranged in a triangular shape. They are incompatible with the two pronged Type C plugs commonly used on the European continent, as UK sockets are shuttered and will not open without the insertion of the third "earth" pin. If travelling from the USA, you will need a power converter or transformer to convert the voltage from 230 to 110, to avoid damage to your appliances. The latest models of certain types of camcorders, cell phones and digital cameras are dual-voltage, which means that they were manufactured with a built in converter, but you will have to check with your dealer about that.

Food & Drink

England gave the world one of its favourite breakfast, the Full English, a hearty feast of bacon eggs, sausage, fried mushroom and grilled tomato. In the UK, this signature dish is incomplete without a helping of baked beans. In Scotland, you can expect to see black pudding or Lorne sausage added to the ensemble, while the Welsh often throw in some cockles or Laverbread.

CARDIFF TRAVEL GUIDE

For simple, basic meals, you cannot go wrong with traditional pub fare. All round favourites include the beef pie, shepherd's pie, bangers and mash and toasted sandwiches. Fish and chips, served in a rolled up sheet of newsprint, is another firm favourite. For Sunday roast, expect an elaborate spread of roasted meat, roasted potatoes, vegetables and Yorkshire pudding. The national dish of Scotland is, of course, Haggis - sheep's offal which is seasoned and boiled in a sheep's stomach. This dish rises to prominence on Burns Night (25 January), when the birthday of the poet Robert Burns is celebrated. Burns wrote 'Address to a Haggis'. The influence of immigrants to the UK has led to kosher haggis (which is 100 percent free of pork products) and an Indian variant, Haggis pakora, said to have originated from the Sikh community. The synergy of Anglo-Indian cuisine also gave rise to popular dishes such as Chicken Tikka Masala and Kedgeree.

The neighbourhood pub is an integral part of social life in the UK and Britain is known for its dark ale, also referred to as bitter. Currently, the most popular beer in the UK is Carling, a Canadian import which has available in the British Isles since the 1980s. Foster's Lager, the second most popular beer in the UK, is brewed by Scottish & Newcastle, the largest brewery in Britain. For a highly rated local brew, raise a mug of award-winning Fuller's beer. The brewery was established early in the 1800s and produces London Pride, London Porter and Chiswick

Bitter, to name just a few. A popular brand from neighbouring Ireland is Guinness. Along with Indian curries, the market share of Indian beer brands like Jaipur or Cobra beer has grown in recent years. Kent has developed as an emergent wine producer.

On the non-alcoholic side, you can hardly beat tea for popularity. The English like to brew it strong and serve it in a warmed china teapot with generous amounts of milk. Tea is served at 11am and 4pm. Afternoon tea is often accompanied with light snacks, such as freshly baked scones or cucumber sandwiches. High tea, served a little later at 6pm, can be regarded as a meal. A mixture of sweet and savoury treats such as cakes, scones, crumpets, cheese or poached egg on toast, cold meats and pickles. The custom of High Tea goes back to the days when dinner was the midday meal. These days, it is often replaced by supper.

Scotland is known for producing some of the world's finest whiskies. Its industry goes back at least 500 years. One of Scotland's best selling single malt whisky is produced by the famous Glenmorangie distillery in the Highlands. Chivas Brothers, who once supplied whisky by royal warrant to Queen Victoria's Scottish household, produce Chivas Regal, one of the best known blended whiskies of Scotland. The Famous Grouse, which is based at Glenturret near the Highlands town of Crieff, produces several excellent examples of blended grain whiskies.

Bell's Whisky is one of the top selling whiskies in the UK and Europe. Other well known Scottish whisky brands include Old Pulteney, Glen Elgin, Tamdhu (a Speyside distillery that produces single malt), Balvenie, Bunnahabhain, Macallan, Aberlour, Bowmore, the award-winning Ballantine and Grant's whisky, from a distillery that has been run by the same family for five generations. Another proudly Scottish drink is Drambuie, the first liqueur stocked by the House of Lords. According to legend, its recipe was originally gifted to the MacKinnon clan by Bonnie Prince Charlie.

Events

Sports

Horse racing is often called the sport of kings and has enjoyed the support of the British aristocracy for centuries. Here you can expect to rub shoulders with high society and several races go back to the 1700s. The Cheltenham Festival is usually on or near St Patrick's Day and now comprises a four day event of 27 races. The Grand National takes place in Liverpool in April. With prize money of £1 million, this challenging event is Europe's richest steeplechase. A Scottish equivalent of the Grand National takes place in Ayr in the same month. There is also a Welsh Grand National, which now takes place in the winter at Chepstow. A past winner of Welsh event was none other than the author Dick Francis. Other important horse races are the Guineas at Newmarket (April/May), the Epsom Oaks and the Epsom Derby (first Saturday of June) and the St Leger Stakes, which takes place in Doncaster in September. One of the annual highlights is Royal Ascot week, traditionally attended by the British Royal Family. This takes place in June at Berkshire. There is a strict dress code and access to the Royal Enclosure is limited, especially for first timers. Fortunately, you will be able to view the the arrival of the monarch in a horse drawn carriage with a full royal procession at the start of the day. Another high profile equestrian event is the St Regis International Polo Cup, which takes place in May at Cowdray Park.

Wimbledon, one of the world's top tennis tournaments, takes place in London from last week of June, through to the first half of July. If you are a golfing enthusiast, do not miss the British Open, scheduled for July at Royal Troon in South Ayrshire, Scotland. The event, which has been played since 1860, is the world's oldest golf tournament. A highlight in motorcycle racing is the Manx Grand Prix, which usually takes place in August or September and serves as a great testing ground for future talent. The British Grand Prix takes place at Silverstone in Northamptonshire. A sporting event that occupies a special place in popular culture is the annual boat race that usually takes place in April between the university teams of Oxford and Cambridge. The tradition goes back to 1829 and draws large numbers of spectators to watch from the banks of the Thames. The FA Cup final, which is played at Wembley Stadium in May, is a must for soccer fans. As a sports event, the London Marathon is over 100 years old and draws entries from around the world to claim its prize money of a million pounds. Keen athletes will only have a brief window period of less than a week to submit their entries. Selection is by random ballot. The 42km race takes place in April.

Cultural

If you want to brush shoulders with some of your favourite authors or get the chance to pitch to a British publisher or agent, you dare not miss the London Book Fair. The event takes place in April and includes talks, panel discussions and exhibitions by a large and diverse selection of publishing role players. The London Art Fair happens in January and features discussions, tours and performances. For comic geeks there are several annual events in the UK to look forward to. The CAPTION comic convention in Oxford, which goes back to the early 1990s, is a must if you want to show your support to Britain's small presses. There is a Scottish Comic Con that takes place in the Edinburgh International Conference Center in April and a Welsh Comic Con, also in April, at Wrexham. The MCM London Comic Con happens over the last weekends of May and October, and covers anime, manga, cosplay, gaming and science fiction in general. The UK's calendar of film festivals clearly shows its cultural diversity. The oldest events are the London Film Festival (October) and the Leeds Film Festival (November). There are also large events in Manchester and Cambridge. The high-profile Encounters festival for shorts and animated films takes place each September in Bristol.

History fans can immerse themselves in the thrills and delights of the Glastonbury Medieval Fayre, which takes place in April and includes stalls, jousting and minstrels. The Tewkesbury Medieval Festival takes place in summer and its key event is the re-enactment of the Battle of Tewkesbury.

Edinburgh has an annual International Film Festival that takes place in June. The city also hosts a broader cultural festival that takes place in August. The Edinburgh International Festival is a three week event that features a packed programme of music, theatre, dance and opera, as well as talks and workshops. The Royal Highland show takes place in June and features agricultural events as well as show jumping. If you want to experience the massing of Scottish pipers, one good opportunity is the Braemar Gathering, an event that takes place on the first Saturday in September and is usually attended by the Royal family. Its roots go back 900 years. Over the spring and summer seasons, you can attend numerous Highland Games, which feature Scottish piping, as well as traditional sports such as hammer throw and tug of war. For Scottish folk dancing, attend the Cowal Highland Gathering, which takes place towards the end of August.

Websites of Interest

http://www.visitbritain.com
http://www.myguidebritain.com/
http://wikitravel.org/en/United_Kingdom
http://www.english-heritage.org.uk/
http://www.celticcastles.com/
http://www.tourist-information-uk.com/

Travel Apps

If you are planning to use public transport around the UK, get Journey Pro to help make the best connections.
https://itunes.apple.com/gb/app/journey-pro-london-uk-by-navitime/id388628933

The Around Me app will help you to orient, if you are looking for the nearest ATM, gas station or other convenience services. http://www.aroundmeapp.com/

If you are worried about missing out on a must-see attraction in a particular area, use the National Trust's app to check out the UK's natural and historical treasures.

http://www.nationaltrust.org.uk/features/app-privacy-policy

Printed in Dunstable, United Kingdom